THE ART OF
GIANCARLO IMPIGLIA

THE ART OF GIANCARLO IMPIGLIA

INTRODUCTION BY

RONNY COHEN

RIZZOLI
NEW YORK

FRONTISPIECE
THE TYCOON ◆ 1988
ACRYLIC ON CANVAS
78″ x 68″

First published in the United States of America in 1995 by
Rizzoli International Publications, Inc.
300 Park Avenue South, New York, New York, 10010

Library of Congress Cataloging-in-Publication Data

Impiglia, Giancarlo.
    The art of Impiglia / by Giancarlo Impiglia ; text by
Ronny Cohen.
        p.   cm.
    ISBN 0–8478–1903–5 (HC)
    l. Impiglia, Giancarlo—Themes, motives. I. Cohen,
Ronny. II. Title.
N6923.I54A4   1995
    760'. 092—dc20   95–15118

DESIGNED BY NAI Y. CHANG

Printed and bound in Italy

ACKNOWLEDGMENTS

Ever since I was a child, I've had a love of design and color. I dreamed of being an artist, particularly a painter. I believe that an artist must first be born an artist, but then also become one through life. I have worked very hard all my life searching for my artistic identity, trying to achieve and fulfill my childhood dream. This drive has directed me to many different artistic disciplines: music, photography, cinematography, painting, and sculpture. This search has also led me to travel throughout Europe, North Africa, India, and, ultimately, across the Atlantic.

The impact of coming to New York for the first time in 1971 was the greatest my Italian soul had ever experienced—it was exciting, dynamic, and breathless all at once. The energy and the atmosphere were absolutely in tune with the work that I was constructing at the time. Dormant Rome, the eternal city with all its beauty, was behind me at that moment. A new chapter of my life was beginning in a different world, a world that faced the future and never looked back. It took a great deal of courage to start life anew on another continent without my family and old friends, but I received a lot of unconditional encouragement and support from my wife, Nina.

Twenty-five years later I am still in New York, still studying and working harder than ever. My artistic vision keeps on growing and the excitement never fades. All of my passion for art has been assembled into this book—twenty-five years of my artistic encounters and discoveries.

I would like to acknowledge and thank all who believed in me. And a greater thanks to all who, in contrast, did not—you made me work harder in order to show how real my dream was.

Rizzoli Bookstores President Antonio Polito and Vice-President John Brancati, whom I have known since 1980, the year I started to exhibit at the Rizzoli galleries in New York, Washington DC, Chicago, and Costa Mesa, California, have made this book possible.

I would like to extend special thanks to Manuela Soares, Senior Editor at Rizzoli Publications, whose skills and creativity made the idea of this book a concrete reality. I would also like to thank the CEO and Publisher, Judith Joseph, who enthusiastically gave the approval to publish *The Art of Giancarlo Impiglia.* And thanks to Nai Y. Chang, the talented designer who, with patience and elegance, transformed a mosaic of images and type into the sophisticated graphic composition of this book. And to writer and critic, Ronny Cohen, I owe a special thanks—I consider her to be the most knowledgeable critic of my work to date. In the 1984 issue of *ArtNews* magazine, she reviewed my show at the Alex Rosenberg Gallery in New York in an article that captured the essence of my work. Through her writing in this book, I am able to review my whole artistic career and convey my experiences. Thanks to Ms. Cohen, the memories of my youth are polished and clear.

I constantly thank my parents for giving me, despite difficulties, my education. I also thank them for giving me life, courage, and ultimately the background that has sustained me throughout my life. I want to thank my older sister, Luciana, for her lifetime support and for saving, until this day, every scrapbook drawing, little painting, and first experiment that she dearly collected ever since I could hold a pencil. And to my brother, Vittorio, with whom I shared a wonderful and fun life as a performer and musician at a time when I couldn't sell my paintings—many thanks.

I am grateful to my wife's parents, Lucille Frand and the late Jay Frand, who enthusiastically welcomed me when I first stepped onto American soil—their encouragement, appreciation, and tremendous support helped make my dream real.

My deepest gratitude goes to my wife of nineteen years, and companion for over twenty-five years, whom I dearly love and respect. She has always believed in me and my work, and has truly been a pillar of my private and artistic life.

I would also like to acknowledge my beautiful children, Thomas and Christopher, who give me the incredible strength to continue and to leave for them a positive legacy.

GIANCARLO IMPIGLIA
NEW YORK CITY
APRIL 3, 1995

TABLE OF
CONTENTS

LIST OF
PLATES

(PAGE NUMBERS PRECEDE TITLES)

I
INTRODUCTION

The penetrating vision of the work of Giancarlo Impiglia provides a compelling portrait of the mood and mores of the twentieth century. From rush hour to cocktail hour; from bustling city streets to serene stretches of beach; from elegant gatherings in opulent penthouses and aboard luxurious ocean liners to intimate romantic encounters on moonlit terraces and posh dance floors—the realities and fantasies of our time and culture are depicted with infinite flair in the colorful compositions and bold images filling Impiglia's paintings. A keen observer, he examines both the ever-passing parade of ordinary workday activities, and the progression of special occasions and celebrations that lend extra dash and sparkle to our existence. What people do, where they go, how they behave—these are the things Impiglia finds endlessly fascinating. For him there is a special challenge in discovery, in finding the new in the familiar. To this task Impiglia applies his formidable talent for interpretation, and establishes himself as a leading chronicler of our actions, hopes, and desires.

Impiglia's acute powers of discernment are strongly evident in all his paintings. He sees things not only for what they are, but also for what they might be. This allows him to be clear and forceful in presenting what he finds to be important, both in the form and idea of things. Paying close attention to surface, shape, and color, he builds compositions from salient details, while treating subjects in terms of their broader implications. Invariably, Impiglia's paintings probe the meaning of human experience. Throughout the series of paintings he began in 1975, a veritable world continues to unfold. It is a fascinating mirror of the world we know—a provocative looking glass held up to the structures, conventions, and ideals of society. In his scrutiny of habits and manners, he invites us to consider the fundamental role that façades play in society. Impiglia shows how façades are used as props by different segments of society.

◆ ◆ ◆

OPPOSITE:
SELF PORTRAIT ◆ 1956
OIL ON CANVAS ◆ 34″ X 24″

Impiglia's interest in the messages encoded in fronts maintained by people and places helps to account for the emphasis on style and design in his work. He encourages us to take a fresh look at twentieth-century style as a critical mainstay of society's major façades. Fashion, for instance, is a key signpost of identity. Impiglia's deep understanding of the whys and wherefores of fashion and the fashionable reverberates through his art. For Impiglia, appearance and illusion are the starting and end points of magic in life and painting. In both of these areas he began his lessons quite early.

Impiglia, who was born in Rome on March 9, 1940, made his initial mark as an artist at the time he was learning to read. He tells a story that underscores his precocious involvement in art: "I have this image in my mind of one of my first teachers in elementary school saying, every morning as I was walking into the classroom, 'Here is Impiglia, our young artist.' " The greeting was sweet to his ears. At six years old, he already considered himself an artist. Impiglia spent hours at the kitchen table copying pictures from comics—Mickey Mouse was a favorite. Clearly, he had a knack for drawing.

During Impiglia's childhood, Italy was rebuilding from the rubble of World War II. Reminders of the war were impossible to miss in his neighborhood of San Giovanni, named after the famous basilica of the Lateran that was nearby. "Sometimes as a kid, I used to walk inside the ruins of buildings which had crumbled from the bombs," he remembers. Life wasn't easy, but it was never dull, especially in a lively household where music was a daily essential. According to Impiglia: "My father was a part-time musician. My uncle, my brother, everybody in my family knew how to play instruments, mostly string instruments." The youngest of three children, he has a brother, Vittorio, and a sister, Luciana. Impiglia also learned to play music, and gravitated to the string bass. As to what made him the only artist in the family, he says: "No one ever told me that I had to draw and paint. It was an instinct."

By the age of fourteen, Impiglia had his own oils and canvases. He devised his own course for studying painting, and modeled his work after that of the painters he admired most—including Paul Cézanne, Amedeo Modigliani, Giorgio de Chirico, Giorgio Morandi, and Carlo Carrà—which he had seen in magazines. During his teenage years, thoughts of painting kept him in a dream-like state. "I was living practically in the clouds. I have memories of walking the streets just looking up at buildings and the sky and imagining how to paint what I was seeing." Already, his preoccupation with looking long and hard at things could be seen in the paintings of those early years.

House (1956) and *Self Portrait* (1957), the two earliest paintings included here, demonstrate Impiglia's careful attention to the representation of appearances. An engaging image of the artist at age seventeen, *Self Portrait* also attests to his admiration for the vigorous painterly legacy of postimpressionism. Although Impiglia has admitted to having Cézanne's self portraits in mind when he executed his own, even in this early example he displays some traits of the artist he will become. The outlines of the face here anticipate the bold linear treatment of figures for which he is known today. The 1958 painting *Landscape* shows him continuing with his self-directed exploration of appearances and postimpressionism.

After finishing "middle school," similar to American high school, Impiglia took a specialized program in photography in Rome. The program taught him about lighting and design in portrait photography, and included classes in the history of photography. This was followed with a program in cinematography, which he took in

HOUSE ◆ 1956
OIL ON CANVAS ◆ 30″ X 24″

Rome at CIAC (Centro Italiano Addestramento Cinematografico). Although the program emphasized the technical side of the industry, it also offered courses in film history. Impiglia explains that his attraction to photography and cinema was part of his general interest in the visual arts. Also, there was the question of making a living to consider. It seemed that compared to painting, photography and cinema offered a broader practical application, and thus, potential employment. Recalling those days, Impiglia says: "I studied the great directors of the Silents, the Russians and Americans, like Vsevolod Pudovkin, Sergei Eisenstein, and D. W. Griffith." He regarded the early twentieth-century films he saw—Eisenstein's *Potemkin* and Griffith's *Birth of a Nation* —as gifts. The impression they made on him opened his eyes, and he treasured them for the knowledge they gave him. Impiglia describes their significance in these terms: "Because of these films, I grew up in my teen years with visions of a big world, not of a small, cloistered world. I became fascinated with all these images. The discovery of this fantastic film world at that age, was incredible to me. All the more so at that time, because in Italy television was only the privilege of the wealthy."

There was, however, a neorealist cinema. And Impiglia was an enthusiastic fan of that powerful expression of 1950s Italian culture, enjoying the work of directors Vittorio De Sica, Roberto Rossellini, and, later on, Federico Fellini, among others. The subject of art was also discussed at the school of cinematography. Impiglia recalls courses exploring art's connections to set design and the dramatic use of art in film, in which the students examined the work of directors like Lucchino Visconti and Michelangelo Antonioni. Contemporary art was another topic that students were likely to discuss as much outside as inside the classroom. "Some of my classmates were sons of artists, art teachers, movie directors, and photographers. They were part of my crowd, and we would go together to all the important exhibitions."

Impiglia frequented galleries such as Galleria La Tartaruga, Galleria dell'Obelisco, L'Attico, and La Salita, which were major showcases for leading contemporary artists from Italy, the United States, and England. When he finished at the school of cinematography, Impiglia had to decide whether to continue in film, which is what a number of his classmates did. He opted not to. "Working in film would have involved teamwork all the time. I wanted to continue my studies in art."

Again picking up the dream of being a painter, he started courses at the Artistic Lyceum, which along with the Accademia Delle Belle Arti formed the "Ferro di Cavallo," the famous block of buildings on Via Ripetta named for its horseshoe shape. This was an important gathering place for artists of all generations in Rome. Many of the major figures in postwar Italian art, from Umberto Mastroianni to Renato Guttuso, taught there. Impiglia had classes with two of the leading painters of the late 1950s, Giulio Turcato and Giuseppe Capogrossi. According to Impiglia: "The

◆ ◆ ◆

program was very broad, with a concentration in art history, and although it was challenging, I was considered advanced in painting when I entered."

There were courses to master in still life and portraiture, technique and materials, design, composition, and architectural drawing. The program continued the venerable academic tradition of having students copy figures from plaster casts. Classical Greek and Roman sculpture, Bernini's *Saint Theresa,* and Michelangelo's *David* were among the examples the students had to reproduce.

While Impiglia was occupied mostly with art of the distant past at the Artistic Lyceum and Accademia delle Belle Arti, he was also an avid follower of the latest contemporary developments in Rome in the late 1950s. He saw the first shows of English figurative painter Francis Bacon at Galleria dell'Obelisco, and American Abstract Expressionist Franz Kline at Galleria La Tartaruga, both in 1958. During this period, one of Impiglia's great favorites was Alberto Burri, one of Italy's leading abstract artists. "I loved Burri, and followed him closely. He was constantly reinventing himself. I especially liked how he used different materials like burlap, wood, and metal, and kept evolving," Impiglia notes. He was intrigued by the connections he saw between Burri and Robert Rauschenberg, another artist he admired for his handling of materials and unusual combinations. Rauschenberg had started showing his work in Rome in the early 1950s, so he was a familiar figure to Impiglia, who privately dubbed him "the American side of Burri."

During this period, Impiglia's exuberant outlook led him to try new things, such as the band he organized with a few of his classmates from the Artistic Lyceum. He chose to play bass, an instrument that was to serve him well. "We were young guys. At first there were three of us, and later five. In a very short time we were pretty successful locally," Impiglia recalls. The band played mostly the popular tunes of the day—songs by Elvis Presley, the Everly Brothers, and the Platters, among others—and performed at parties and nightclubs in Rome. Music indeed proved the source of Impiglia's interest in the pleasures of nightlife, a subject that he would explore insightfully in his painting after 1975. In the band, Impiglia played late into the night, then attended art classes during the day. It was a demanding schedule, and one he maintained for about four years. Then, as the band reached greater levels of success, it required more of his time. They made records, and appeared on Italian television and in Italian movies. "From Capri to the island of Elba, we played in the best, most luxurious resorts all over Italy. It was *la dolce vita,* lots of fun, an exciting way to make a living," says Impiglia.

His growing renown as a musician presented him with a dilemma concerning his art. His musical obligations forced him to stop taking art classes. Still, he had no intention of abandoning either the dream of being a full-time painter or his need to keep up with the latest developments in contemporary art. Whenever he worked on tour as a musician—in Tunisia where he spent a year and a half during the mid-1960s, and in England where he performed in 1967–68—Impiglia always brought oils and canvases along. He continued to make paintings when he could find the time. In London, instead of going to music stores, he spent much of his free time looking at art. He was a frequent visitor to the Tate Gallery and British Museum, and attended the gallery exhibitions of artists like Francis Bacon and pop painter Andy Warhol, whose work he had first seen in Rome.

In 1968, a year of student and worker strikes and demonstrations in Italy, and unrest and division in the United States and elsewhere, Impiglia decided to start initiating changes in his own life as well. He stopped touring and returned to Rome, determined to make more time for painting. Combining his interests in music and art, he opened a studio specializing in images for vocal artists and record companies. "From record covers, logos, and book jackets, to ads, posters, and illustrations, I did it all. I had to call upon my photographic skills as well." His work schedule allowed time for his personal work, and soon he was directing his attentions toward *arte povera,* the major Italian art movement of the late 1960s.

Arte povera or "poor art," a term coined by Italian art critic Germano Celant, referred to art that employed rough, ordinary, and non-traditional materials. Impiglia knew a number of artists associated with this movement, including Mario Schifano, Franco Angeli, and Tano Festa; some had been in art school with him. He explains the movement's appeal to him: "I found the idea of giving values to things like old clothes and found objects very poetic." He produced his first works about fashion in 1968 with *Reflections of Wealth* and *Mother Nature,* in which he combined actual pairs of jeans and other clothing items using the freedom of expression he found in *arte povera.* Impiglia showed that fashion was a symbolic language of 1960s culture, used to bond, identify, and separate the younger generation from its elders and express basic messages ("Make Love, Not War," "Back To Nature") of the then-burgeoning youth culture.

In 1970, Impiglia was asked by a friend to go on a photojournalism assignment to Bangladesh. The challenge of applying his photography in a new way appealed to him, and he agreed. Impiglia recalls: "We went by car overland from Rome, across Yugoslavia, Bulgaria, Turkey, Iran, Afghanistan, Pakistan, and through India and Nepal. There were soldiers, people shooting. I didn't want anything to do with guns and bullets, and decided to photograph landscapes. One day when I was taking a picture from a bridge, a soldier came along and, without warning, put a gun to my neck. I thought my life was finished. There were dangerous moments, risks everywhere. It was an absolutely frightening, but important experience."

Impiglia considers the six months he spent as a photojournalist an invaluable part of an education in what he has termed "the school of life."

In between jobs that took him away from Rome, Impiglia continued making paintings and assemblages in the experimental spirit inspired by *arte povera.* In 1971, he was seeking an advanced degree in this field when he made his first trip to New York. One night in Rome, a club owner from New York heard him playing, and asked

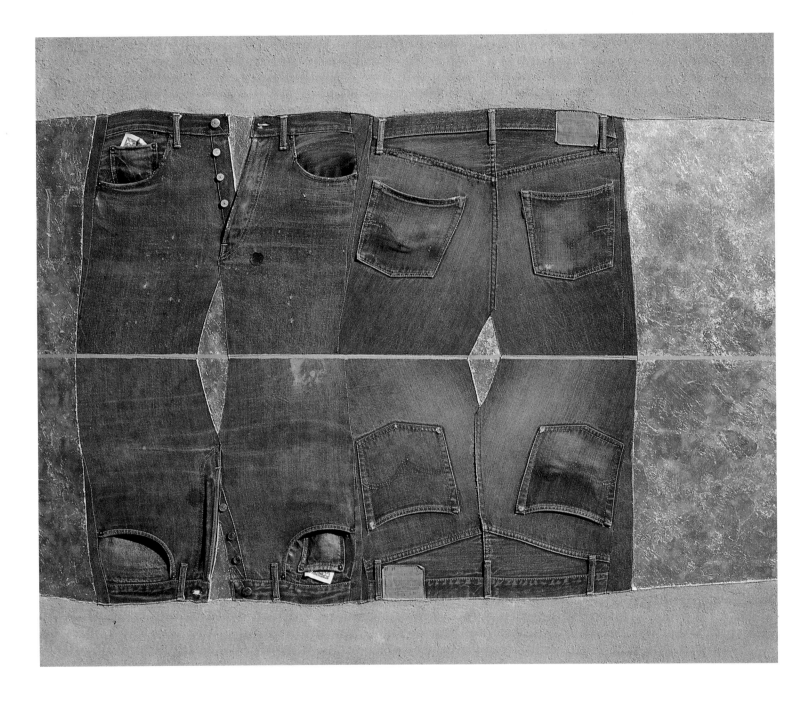

REFLECTIONS OF WEALTH ◆ 1968
ASSEMBLAGE ◆ 42″ X 54″

MOTHER NATURE ◆ 1968
OIL, ACRYLIC, AND GOLD LEAF MOUNTED ON CANVAS
61″ X 71″

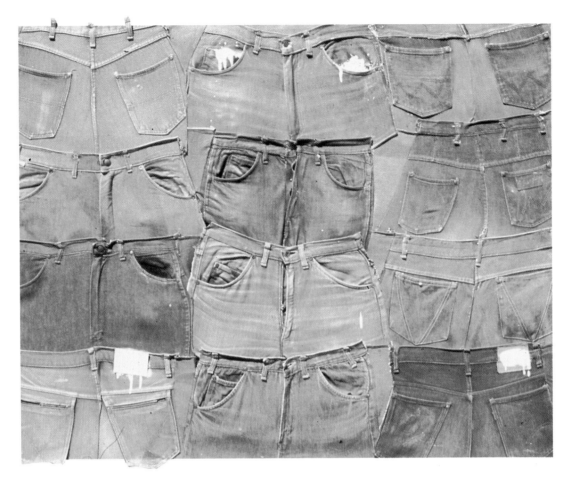

MULTITUDE ◆ 1973
ASSEMBLAGE ◆ 44″ X 55″

if he and his brother, who also played in the band, would be interested in working in New York for six months. "So my brother and I broke up the band in Rome. I closed my studio. This was a great opportunity to see New York and the United States. Two weeks later we were there." New York made a terrific first impression. He spent his first evening doing what he had done as a boy in Rome—walking back and forth and looking around the streets, ever the observer. "All those lights and buildings and people at every hour, it was fascinating." He also reconnected with his future wife, Nina Frand, whom he had first met in Italy.

In New York, Impiglia was struck by the contrasts to Rome. In the Rome he had left behind, lights were dimmed at night, and life went on at a slower pace. In addition to visiting museums and galleries and performing music, he set himself the task of discerning the main features of what he called "a different kind of society in New York."

Impiglia focused on the activities and energies of the streets. After he was back in Rome, he thought about his stay in New York and the significance it had for him. "It made me change my way of looking at what I was doing with *arte povera*, although I did not immediately stop working with the idea of clothing and costume."

Multitudes, which he produced in Rome in 1973, continued his explorations of the sociological and political symbolism of blue jeans, shown as the preferred uniform of the contemporary masses. It is interesting to note how the crowd, one of the underlying concerns in *Multitudes*, re-emerges as a major theme in the urban landscape paintings that followed Impiglia's *arte povera* period. By the time he completed the last of the *arte povera* pieces, Impiglia had begun work on a new visual language that he would develop in the urban landscape paintings, and all of his future work.

Impiglia's desire to invent a new form of representation was based in New York. Toward the end of his stay, he had been asked to submit a study for a sixty-foot mural painting for the lobby of Ninety-nine John Street in the Wall Street area. He won the commission with two small paintings he had worked on in Rome. This commission was large enough to make it economically feasible for him to return to New York and begin to realize the dream of being a full-time, self-supporting artist.

In the summer of 1973, he and Nina, who had joined him in Italy, moved to New York. The mural he worked on for the next year, *Revisiting Lower Manhattan*, marked the debut of his neo-deco paintings. Impiglia arrived at the boldly simplified figures and forms he called neo-deco through a creative interpretation of the early twentieth-century style known as Art Deco, and through seeing the Art Deco buildings and lamp posts of the 1920s and 1930s still standing in Manhattan and the surrounding boroughs in the early 1970s. Impiglia uses this method of combining analysis and reconstruction of the language of art, with lessons learned from "the school of life," to give striking expression to the humanistic concerns and values at the core of his art of the last two decades.

In what he calls "my quest for myself," Impiglia discovers the dimensions of his vision, and asks us to stretch our own boundaries, as his painting renews our faith in the enchanting, enlightening, and exciting beauty of art.

RONNY COHEN
NEW YORK CITY

GIANCARLO IMPIGLIA 1980©

II
URBAN LIFE

Soon after moving to New York in 1973, Impiglia began registering the city's strong impact on him. In New York, he encountered the ultra urban experience, what he has called "the city projected into the future." Crowds, buildings, and huge department stores were among the things that made a powerful first impression. "I was fascinated by the escalators at places like Macy's and Bloomingdale's, this crush of people moving up and down," Impiglia says. His remark helps us understand his intentions in *Escalator,* part of the early group of work in which he set forth the expressive character of the *Urban Life* series.

Over the last two decades Impiglia has focused on images of people perpetually on the go. These examples reveal his deep appreciation of the sense of motion and mobility that so thoroughly permeates contemporary city life. Directing a sharp eye to the streets and avenues shaping the flow of this movement, he has succeeded in turning daily activities like walking, window shopping, and commuting into monumental endeavors. Examples like *Movimenti Simultanei* reveal his deep interest in Italian Futurism, and the analytical depictions of motion found in the work of such leading artists of the movement as Giacomo Balla, Umberto Boccioni, Gino Severini, and Fortunato Depero.

In appealing representations blending reality and fantasy, Impiglia forges his signature style. The bold synthesis of recognizable and abstract elements, perhaps most compelling in the deliberately blank faces, encourages us to look beyond surface appearances.

◆ ◆ ◆

OPPOSITE:
MADISON AVENUE ◆ 1980
ACRYLIC ON CANVAS ◆ 60″ x 50″

RIGHT:
WORKERS ◆ 1975
ACRYLIC ON CANVAS ◆ 61″ x 43″

OPPOSITE:
BUS STOP ◆ 1975
ACRYLIC ON CANVAS ◆ 50″ x 40″

OPPOSITE:
SIGNS ◆ 1975
ACRYLIC ON CANVAS ◆ 48″ x 38″

ABOVE:
THE BAR ◆ 1976
ACRYLIC ON CANVAS ◆ 41″ x 61″

27

ESCALATOR ◆ 1975
ACRYLIC ON CANVAS ◆ 61″ x 43″

ESCALATOR ◆ 1980
ACRYLIC ON CANVAS ◆ 55½″ x 40½″

5:05 ◆ 1980

PENCIL ON VELLUM ◆ 13⅛″ x 11¼″

DON'T WALK ◆ 1980
ACRYLIC ON CANVAS
71" x 60"

PAGES 32-33
TICKET HOLDERS
(QUEUING) ◆ 1981
ACRYLIC ON PAPER
30" x 60"

GIANCARLO IMPIGLIA 81

"WINDOW SHOPPING" SKETCH FOR A PAINTING

ABOVE:
WINDOW SHOPPING ◆ 1981
PENCIL ON VELLUM ◆ 26″ x 21″

OPPOSITE:
WINDOW SHOPPING ◆ 1981
ACRYLIC ON CANVAS ◆ 56″ x 48″

THE LAST TRAIN
1983
PASTEL ON VELLUM
7⅛″ x 15¼″

THE LAST TRAIN   ◆   1983
ACRYLIC ON WOOD   ◆   42″ x 84″

IN STEP ◆ 1982
ACRYLIC ON CANVAS ◆ 35½″ x 47½″

GIANCARLO IMPIGLIA 1985

PARK AVENUE SOUTH ◆ 1985
ACRYLIC ON CANVAS ◆ 48″ x 72″

CITY PULSE 88 ◆ 1988
PASTEL ON CANVAS ◆ 48″ x 72″

LEFT:
CROWD ◆ 1987
PASTEL ON BOARD ◆ 11½" x 19⅜"

BELOW:
LIFE IN THE CITY ◆ 1987
ACRYLIC ON CANVAS ◆ 42" x 60"

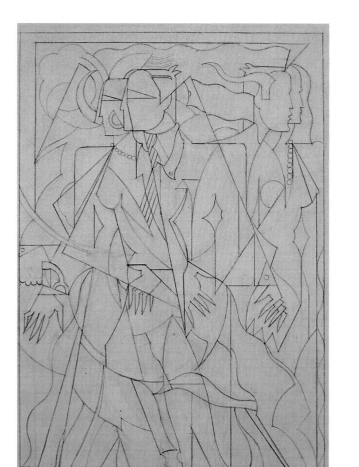

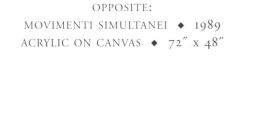
OPPOSITE:
MOVIMENTI SIMULTANEI ◆ 1989
ACRYLIC ON CANVAS ◆ 72″ x 48″

ABOVE:
MOVIMENTI SIMULTANEI ◆ 1989
PENCIL ON PAPER ◆ 14½″ x 9¾″

RIGHT:
MOVIMENTI SIMULTANEI ◆ 1989
PASTEL ON VELLUM ◆ 14½″ x 9¾″

III
UNDER
THE SUN

"For me these works are about taking a break from the city. In the summer I like to go somewhere more peaceful," Impiglia says, referring to his beach and country scenes. During this time, he explores more idyllic themes and interests than the active pace of his New York-based life and career can possibly allow. Examples from this period show Impiglia's contributions to the rich tradition of symbolic figure painting in twentieth-century art. From Henri Matisse to Pablo Picasso to Giorgio de Chirico, artists practicing a diversity of styles have enjoyed the challenge of embodying emblematic meanings ranging from feelings of love and desire to ideas about history and culture, in humanized form. Impiglia takes pleasure in fully exercising his imagination to meet this challenge.

The figures we find in *Beach Games* and the two *Laguna Beach* examples seem at once familiar and dreamily removed. They are the quintessential "California Girls" of legend and song, with toned bodies in keeping with 1990s standards of workouts and well-being. They are touched, however, with the brush of heroic idealism, and also bring to mind the nymphs and goddesses of myth and legend.

◆ ◆ ◆

OPPOSITE:
BEACH GAMES ◆ 1985
ACRYLIC ON CANVAS ◆ 40″ x 52″

47

A DAY AT THE RACES I ◆ 1985
PASTEL ON BOARD ◆ 33″ x 43″

ABOVE:
A DAY AT THE RACES II ◆ 1985
PASTEL ON BOARD ◆ 33″ x 43″

PAGE 50:
HARVEST TIME ◆ 1990
PASTEL ON BOARD ◆ 84″ x 72″

PAGE 51:
BUSTLING ◆ 1990
PASTEL ON BROWN PAPER ◆ 36¾″ x 34″

GIANCARLO IMPIGLIA ©1990

ABOVE:
LAGUNA BEACH (SUNBATHERS) ◆ 1991
COLORED PENCIL ON PAPER ◆ 7½″ x 6½″

OPPOSITE:
LAGUNA BEACH (SUNBATHERS) ◆ 1991
ACRYLIC ON CANVAS ◆ 54″ x 46″

IV
THE HIGH LIFE

Drawing on his many lessons in "the school of life," Impiglia creates some of his most unforgettable images in this series devoted to elegance and romance. Here we are given front row, grand tier seats to see the manners and pleasures of society. Impiglia consciously evokes the Art Deco period of the 1920s and 1930s, in which standards of refinement reached new heights in formal fashion, luxury design, and stylish behavior. *Intermission,* a perfectly balanced composition based on oppositions, reveals Impiglia's mastery of the principles of contrast and repetition favored by leading Art Deco graphic designers like A. M. Cassandre.

In *Night Rhythm* and *Party Time,* two vibrant showcases for the playful, sensual energies of the dance floor, Impiglia continues his investigation of motion. Like a film director, he succeeds in establishing both the look and the feeling of a place. Comparisons with film seem appropriate in view of Impiglia's sophisticated use of close-ups and multiple actions in a single scene. He even uses art in his settings—as Russian director Sergei Eisenstein might have done—as an expressive device to comment on actions and characters.

In *The Grand Party,* for example, the frescos in the vaulted ceiling have faces. Which are real, the frescos or the figures? Where does illusion begin and end? What kinds of people are beneath the beautiful façades of tuxedos and gowns? Only Impiglia knows for sure.

◆ ◆ ◆

OPPOSITE:
THE GRAND PARTY ◆ 1985
ACRYLIC ON CANVAS ◆ 96″ x 121″

ABOVE:
MARTINI GLASS ◆ 1993
ACRYLIC ON BOARD ◆ 12″ x 14″

EVERYDAY ◆ 1983
ACRYLIC ON CANVAS
46" x 32"

DRESSING UP ◆ 1984
ACRYLIC ON CANVAS ◆ 34″ x 48″

LEFT:
INTERMISSION ◆ 1980
7–COLOR SILKSCREEN ◆ 23½" x 17"

OPPOSITE:
ALLEGRO ◆ 1981
ACRYLIC ON CANVAS ◆ 34" x 30"

STUDY FOR SKY PARTY ◆ 1981
PASTEL ON VELLUM ◆ 42″ x 74″

ABOVE:
SPARKLING NIGHT ◆ 1988
ACRYLIC ON CANVAS ◆ 32″ x 36″

OPPOSITE:
THE KISS ◆ 1983
ACRYLIC ON CANVAS ◆ 30″ x 24″

FANTASY ◆ 1986
ACRYLIC ON CANVAS ◆ 60″ x 42″

DREAMLIKE ◆ 1986
ACRYLIC ON CANVAS ◆ 60" x 42"

ABOVE:
NIGHT RHYTHM I ◆ 1988
WHITE CHALK ON BLACK PAPER ◆ 84″ x 45½″

RIGHT:
NIGHT RHYTHM II ◆ 1988
PASTEL ON BLACK PAPER ◆ 84″ x 45½″

CLOSE UP ◆ 1988
ACRYLIC ON CANVAS ◆ 27½″ x 38″

GIANCARLO IMPIGLIA © 1988

LEFT:
SMALL TALK ◆ 1988
ACRYLIC ON CANVAS
48″ x 36½″

OPPOSITE:
THE TYCOON ◆ 1988
ACRYLIC ON CANVAS
78″ x 68″

FIGURE MULTIPLE ◆ 1989
ACRYLIC ON CANVAS ◆ 60" x 42"

RIGHT:
TALKING HEADS IV
(DETAIL) ◆ 1988
WHITE CHALK ON BLACK PAPER
36″ x 96″

PAGES 72-73:
TALKING HEADS ◆ 1988
SILKSCREEN PRINT ◆ 17¾″ x 40″

ABOVE:
PARTY TIME ◆ 1989
PENCIL ON VELLUM ◆ 7½″ x 11″

RIGHT:
PARTY TIME ◆ 1989
ACRYLIC ON CANVAS ◆ 66″ x 102″

MOONLIT WEDDING ◆ 1993
PENCIL ON VELLUM ◆ 10¼″ x 14½″

76

MOONLIT WEDDING ◆ 1993
ACRYLIC ON MASONITE ◆ 10¼″ x 14½″

V
COMPANIONS

In the group he calls "Companions," Impiglia creates a new context for his images. *A Taste of Life, The Appointment, Sunbather,* and *Running Late* demonstrate the range of the cutout paintings. Painted front and back, the cutouts are mostly lifesize versions of what appear to be details from Impiglia's other paintings. Some figures are taken directly from series like "Urban Life," "The High Life," and the commissioned works in "Patrons of The Arts," and others are very similar in spirit, but independently conceived. In the cutouts, Impiglia allows the figures to step out of the canvas paintings and into three-dimensional space. They physically enter our surroundings—art enters life. In this respect, the cutouts can be compared to earlier *arte povera* paintings and assemblages in which Impiglia included blue jeans and other clothing articles. *Overalls,* the first of the cutouts, illustrates this connection. In the cutouts, Impiglia also explores his sense of the figures' reality. In this format, he can develop "their individual characters."

Almost all of the cutouts have strong narrative aspects. They appear to express a specific moment, whether a celebration in *A Taste of Life,* or the anticipation of a rendezvous in *The Appointment.* Their capacity to make us smile at them like friends is a measure of the strong imaginative qualities Impiglia has invested in them.

◆ ◆ ◆

OPPOSITE:
A TASTE OF LIFE ◆ 1991
ACRYLIC AND GOLD LEAF ON WOOD ◆ LIFESIZE

59TH AND 3RD ◆ 1980
ACRYLIC ON WOOD ◆ LIFESIZE

80

THE APPOINTMENT ◆ 1980
ACRYLIC ON WOOD ◆ LIFESIZE

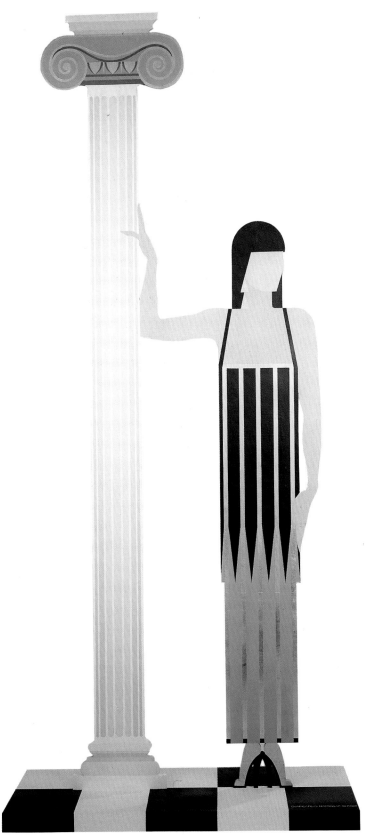

OPPOSITE:
OVERALLS ◆ 1980
ACRYLIC ON WOOD ◆ LIFESIZE

THE CLASSIC TOUCH ◆ 1980
ACRYLIC ON WOOD ◆ LIFESIZE

LEFT:
DIALOGUE ◆ 1980
ACRYLIC ON WOOD ◆ LIFESIZE

OPPOSITE:
CONVERSATION ◆ 1980
ACRYLIC ON WOOD ◆ LIFESIZE

SUNBATHER, 1980
FRONT AND BACK
ACRYLIC ON WOOD ◆ LIFESIZE

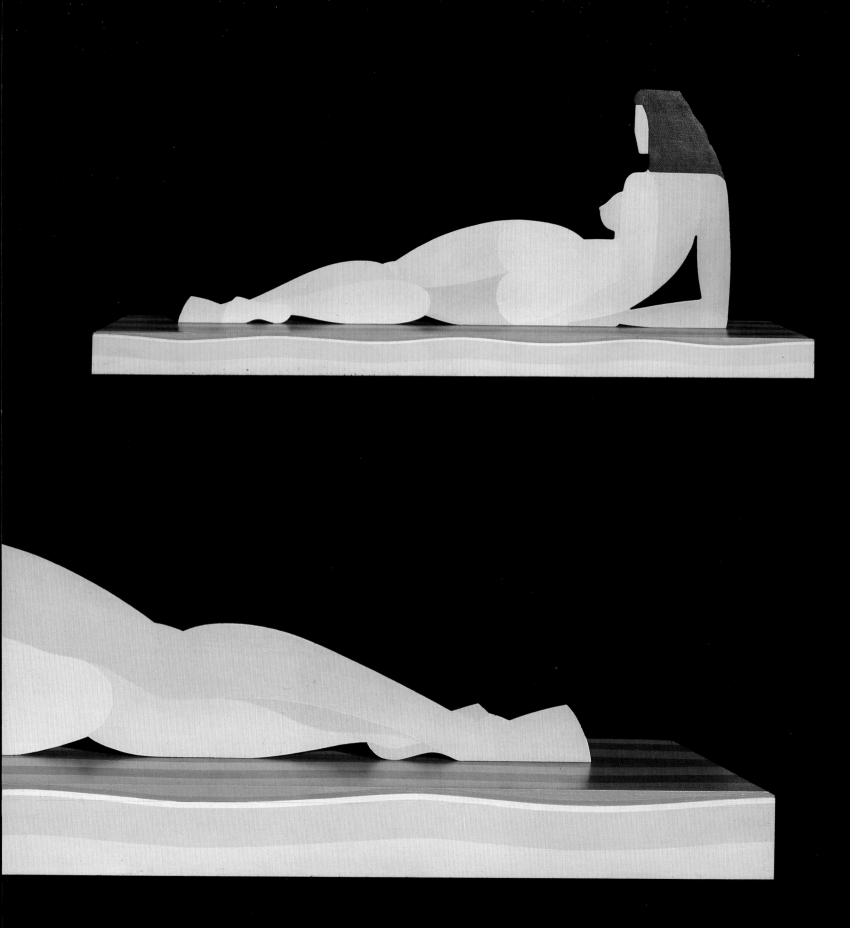

LEFT:
THE ARISTOCRATS II ◆ 1992
ACRYLIC ON WOOD ◆ LIFESIZE

OPPOSITE:
THE DOOR OF YOUR DREAMS ◆ 1991
ACRYLIC AND GOLD LEAF ON WOOD
SCULPTURE AND PAINTING
51″ X 108″ X 10″

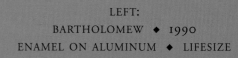

LEFT:
BARTHOLOMEW ◆ 1990
ENAMEL ON ALUMINUM ◆ LIFESIZE

OPPOSITE:
ANOTHER KISS ◆ 1987
ACRYLIC ON WOOD ◆ LIFESIZE

RUNNING LATE ◆ 1990
FRONT AND BACK
ACRYLIC ON WOOD ◆ LIFESIZE

VI
PATRONS OF THE ARTS

Impiglia welcomes commissions and the special challenges they entail. While a patron might know the location he or she wants a painting to hang, or have an idea about the subject, Impiglia determines the concept and approach. For *Revisiting Lower Manhattan*, a five-panel wall mural for his first major commission, Impiglia proposed a vision of New York in the early 1930s, the same era in which the building was constructed. He recalls how the commission that produced *The Top of the City* began with a visit to the patron's apartment. "I saw the space. It had high ceilings and big walls. I imagined a palatial setting. That's what led me to that image." Impiglia's grand composition, his first large painting on the "High Life" theme, made a perfect addition to the Fifth Avenue penthouse in which it is displayed. The Cafe Society panels offered a different challenge in the form of a large-scale work for a restaurant. "I saw this enormous space. Construction had only just started. They were pouring the concrete for the floor," Impiglia recalls. The owners wanted a thirty-five-foot-long painting. He met the demanding size requirements with five seven-by-seven-foot panels representing the restaurant's lavish theme in an impressive panorama of elegant nightclub life.

When Impiglia first saw the Queen Elizabeth II, the ocean liner was about to be sent off for refurbishing. "I walked around the empty decks and began thinking about the good times people have aboard this huge ship." In *Lifestyle I* and *II*, Impiglia offers the passengers of the Queen Elizabeth II a magnificent looking glass reflecting the pleasures of the luxurious ocean liner.

◆ ◆ ◆

OPPOSITE:
ABSOLUT IMPIGLIA ◆ 1992
ACRYLIC AND GOLD LEAF ON MASONITE ◆ 33″ x 31″
COMMISSION FOR ABSOLUT VODKA

REVISITING LOWER MANHATTAN (PANEL II) ◆ 1975
ACRYLIC ON CANVAS ◆ 5′ x 13′
COMMISSION FOR 99 JOHN STREET, NEW YORK CITY

REVISITING LOWER MANHATTAN
(PANEL IV) ◆ 1976
ACRYLIC ON CANVAS
6′ x 9′ ◆ COMMISSION FOR
99 JOHN STREET,
NEW YORK CITY

THE TOP OF THE CITY (PANEL I)
1981 ◆ ACRYLIC ON CANVAS
10′ X 7′
COMMISSION FOR FORTUNOFF

THE TOP OF THE CITY (PANEL II)
1981 ◆ ACRYLIC ON CANVAS
10′ X 7′
COMMISSION FOR FORTUNOFF

LEFT:
FIFTH AVENUE REVISITED (DETAIL) ◆ 1979
ACRYLIC ON CANVAS ◆ FULL SIZE OF PAINTING 8′ x 37′
COMMISSION FOR FORTUNOFF

OPPOSITE:
SILK STOCKING ◆ 1982
ACRYLIC ON CANVAS ◆ 4´ x 7´
COMMISSION FOR PRIVATE RESIDENCE

BELOW:
THE BIG BAND, FIVE PANEL MURAL ◆ 1987
ACRYLIC ON CANVAS ◆ 7´ x 35´
COMMISSION FOR CAFE SOCIETY

MIDSUMMER'S NIGHT PARTY (THREE PANELS) ◆ 1989
ACRYLIC ON CANVAS ◆ 6´ x 18´
COMMISSION FOR PRIVATE RESIDENCE

21 STATE ◆ 1993
ACRYLIC ON CANVAS ◆ 6′ x 10′
COMMISSION FOR FIFTH / THIRD BANK,
COLUMBUS, OHIO

THE FLIGHT ◆ 1992
ACRYLIC ON CANVAS ◆ 4′ x 7′
COMMISSION FOR USAIR

GIANCARLO IMPIGLIA ©1992

111

VALET PARKING ◆ 1989
ACRYLIC ON CANVAS ◆ 5′ x 7′
COMMISSION FOR PRIVATE RESIDENCE

PAGES 114–19:
MURALS FOR
QUEEN ELIZABETH II
COMMISSION FOR CUNARD

LEFT:
LIFE STYLE I ◆ 1994
BLACK AND WHITE SKETCH
13″ x 34″

PAGES 114–15:
LIFE STYLE I ◆ 1994
ACRYLIC ON CANVAS ◆ 13′ x 5′

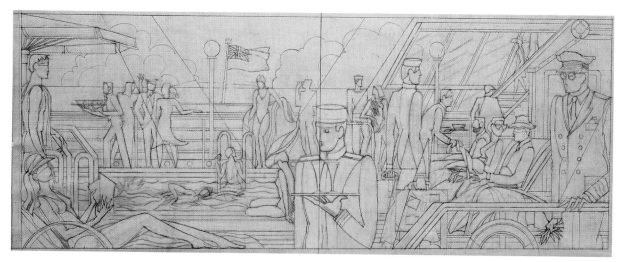

LEFT:
LIFE STYLE II ◆ 1994
BLACK AND WHITE SKETCH
13″ x 34″

PAGES 116–17:
LIFE STYLE II ◆ 1994
ACRYLIC ON CANVAS ◆ 13′ x 5′

LEFT:
HENLEY REGATTA ◆ 1994
BLACK AND WHITE SKETCH
35½″ x 98½″

PAGES 118–19
HENLEY REGATTA ◆ 1994
ACRYLIC ON CANVAS
35½″ x 98½″

VII
NEW DIRECTIONS

Impiglia's commitment to the values he holds most dear is the engine driving his vision into new formal and thematic territories.

It is imperative that the art Impiglia makes be positive and constructive in outlook. He is philosophically opposed to "the constant negativism in contemporary art, this concept of destroying old values to create new values. . . . It is necessary to reconstruct and not destroy, to find continuity and values in culture." This viewpoint accounts for the enthusiasm with which he highlights the fundamental meanings in his work. He also believes in the value of form in art—concept alone is not enough. This belief is reflected in the abstract paintings in which he investigates color, shape, and line, free from the demands of representation. *Kaleidoscope* and *Fragments* reveal the strong sense of geometry underlining his figurative work. In *Kaleidoscope,* his interest in interpreting light through color can be seen in the patterns created by sparkling reds, pinks, and yellows.

Impiglia demonstrates a continuity of concerns that have long been part of his career in *Warlords* and *Night Warriors,* two works that represent the start of a new series. In these works, he relocates the elegant figures we would expect to find in "The High Life" paintings to a new medium—camouflage fabric. With this fabric, he encourages us to think about the significance of this additional façade on the previously established fronts, both physical and social, of these apparently

◆ ◆ ◆

OPPOSITE:
NIGHT WARRIORS ◆ 1994
ACRYLIC ON CAMOUFLAGE ◆ 48″ x 36″

ABOVE:
KALEIDOSCOPE ◆ 1993
ACRYLIC AND GOLD LEAF ON CANVAS ◆ 36″ x 72″

122

PAGE 124:
KALEIDOSCOPE ♦ 1989
ACRYLIC AND GOLD LEAF ON CANVAS ♦ 84″ x 72″

PAGE 125:
FRAGMENTS ♦ 1990
ACRYLIC AND GOLD LEAF ON CANVAS ♦ 72″ x 60″

WARLORDS ◆ 1994
ACRYLIC ON CAMOUFLAGE
40″ x 72″